REDESIGN YOUR LIFE

MAKE EACH DAY YOUR MASTERPICE

PADMA PAVANI NUDURUPATI

Made with ♥ on the Notion Press Platform
www.notionpress.com

This book is dedicated to my late parents whose love for me laid the foundation of who I am today.

Contents

Preface

My ultimate belief in life is that everyone needs happiness irrespective of who they are. Not being happy might be in one or more areas of our lives. Unfortunately, we as humans concentrate on one area and ignore the other essential aspects of our life, which turns into a bigger problem in later stages. Everyone needs a life of fulfillment.

In this book, I have given scientific and spiritual tested and proven techniques to improve all areas of our life. After reading each chapter, one must implement all the methods, notice the difference, and it should be journaled. Journaling our thoughts and progress will register things in our subconscious mind. Trying out these methods for at least 21 days will give us enough progress and drive that will compel us to continue implementing them for the next 90 days to make it a part of our nature. Then, we can naturally become happy and experience balance in all areas of our life. Our physical, social, financial, and relationship are interrelated to our mental health. If we are not optimistic even in a single area, it creates ripples and disturbs other regions. Highly successful people in society are spiritually strong to achieve their goals and face challenges effortlessly to fulfill their purpose in life. I have given powerful mantras to develop relationship, physical, financial, spiritual, and mental health in this book.

I hope you will have a good time reading my first book.

"Only Love and Power to the World"

Acknowledgements

In my spiritual journey, I experienced love, care, contentment, and joy. I sincerely thank the almighty authority for his gracious support and the strength he's given me to face challenges.

I am dedicating this book to my parents and my heartful gratitude wherever they are. I used to think about my father incorrectly, as he was a furious man. However, I experienced his love and affection after my marriage. He was always there for me and supported me in every step of my life. And my special gratitude to my mother, who instilled many virtues in me. Her love, affection, and support made me what I am today. Unfortunately, I lost both of my parents in the past few months.

I sincerely thank my loving husband, Ramesh, and children, Manila and Akhila. Because of their love and support, I was able to turn this book from mind to reality.

I want to devote special thanks to my brother Santosh. I learned the meaning of "MY Word is My Bond" from him. He wrote a letter at the age of 22 stating that he would always be there for me no matter what. To date, he kept his word. I equally thank my siblings Sukanya and Sowjanya. My childhood would not be so wonderful without them. I also thank my extended family. And special thanks to my nieces Aashika and Chaitrika for their love.

I want to express my gratitude to all my Gurus. My special thanks to Mr. GK, who introduced me to the "Law of Attraction" concept. I want to recognize and express my gratitude to some people I have never met, whose lives work, and speeches have impacted me (BK Shivani, Gaur Gopal Das, Mahatrai, Sadh guru, Pandit Sri Ravishankar jee, Mitesh Khatri, Robin Sharma, Tony Robins, Napoleon Hill) with such a force that I cannot let this moment pass. They have helped me connect with my inner self and guided me to release all past emotional baggage, seek the clarity to experience the present, and live a self-aware/meaningful life by only spreading love and light to others.

I would also include thanks to a lot of wonderful people and friends who touched my life in different ways.

Last but not least, my deepest gratitude to the most amazing people dating centuries back, who compiled the secret knowledge so that we can weave this magic and transform our lives.

Prologue

Getting the book started with a profound real-life situation:

A small situation between a father and daughter is an eye-opener for us. One day, a girl went up to her father and said she was bored and asked him to play with her, but he said he was reading a newspaper and would play with her later. Then her father found a world map in the newspaper that he was reading and tore it into pieces. He said if she could join the torn pieces to form a perfect world map, he would play with her. Of course, the father knew that she won't be able to do it, as he couldn't. Still, to his surprise, she approached him after a few minutes, saying she had completed the map. He was surprised and asked how she did it. She said that behind the world map, there was a human figure. She said she didn't know how to make a world map but did know how to make a human correctly. When she joined the pieces of the human figure together, the map was also completed. This left father stunned. Father realizes his daughter's words

"When I corrected the human figure, The world became correct."

I learned a new perspective of life that the world cannot be changed how I like it. However, it is easy to change myself according to this world. I understood that My life is never dependent on what is happening in the outside world. It ultimately depends on the world inside me, which means my thoughts, feelings, emotions, beliefs, habits, and actions only create one's life. If I work on my feelings, emotions, beliefs and actions, can change my life however I want to.

I came to know about the Law of Attraction. I was shocked to learn a few facts. The Law of attraction is not a philosophy, but science like Law of Gravity. What we have in our life is because of what we attract, and that attraction has a frequency. Many of us, use it unknowingly and attract positive and negative circumstances.

We sometimes don't know the universal laws of nature, so we only attract what we don't want.

The Law of attraction always works like Law of Gravity. Let me brief you about gravity; before NEWTON discovered Earth had gravitational force, objects reached the surface when something was thrown in the air. In the same way, whether we accept or not, whether we use it consciously or unconsciously, whether we do it knowingly or unknowingly, we use techniques of the Law of attraction- we attract things, situations, and persons in our life. As per the Law of Attraction, everything you need/want is available in this Universe abundantly. Therefore, we should know how to ask, what to ask for and how to receive it.

One day, while I was delivering the concept of Law of attraction in my training session, one of my students realized his mistake of attracting the wrong things in his life; unknowingly, he attracted what he didn't want. He has a friend with enormous wealth paying high wealth tax, and his friend proudly shares the same with him. He was also passionate about paying more taxes like him. He used to think I would also pay taxes like him one day. So, he attracted what he wanted, and the government increased wealth taxes twice in the same year, fulfilling his wish. His intention was to accumulate more wealth and how much his friend had. But instead, he attracted taxes.

The Universe understands only one language, the language of feelings. Everything is made up of energy; every energy has its own frequency, and when frequency matches, attraction happens. As it is a profound subject, I am trying to guide and educate the root cause of negative feelings, emotions, beliefs, and disempowering actions, which are causing to attract negatives into your life. By implementing the learnings from this book, you can attract positive results in all areas of your life. Mainly concentrating on mental, relationships, physical, financial, and spiritual health. I will also mention all scientifical evidence to establish the points I discuss.

CHAPTER I

Acceptance

"Acceptance looks like a passive state, but in reality, it brings something entirely new into this world. That peace, a subtle energy vibration, is consciousness"

By Eckhart Tolle

One of the leading causes of heart disease is down to- too much stress. One of the best ways to reduce stress is to accept the things you cannot control. Realistic thinking helps reduce the unnecessary fear of not being in total control. After all, it's impossible to control every single aspect of our lives. So why feed your fears? Attaching your sense of self to a false view of reality can be psychologically damaging in the long run. Acceptance is a powerful tool. The people around you and the situations in your life do not make you feel negative. It is your thought process that makes you feel the negativity. From the time you start accepting your reality, you become a positive person. For example, when you are in a hurry leaving to office, and your wife/mom spills water on your pant, you tend to get angry. Consider the same thing happening in a meeting hall in front of delegates and your boss. You never get mad, instead you smile and say it's okay. When something has happened or is about to happen, which is not the way you wished for, you tend to get angry, but when you accept the situation, you will tolerate it.

Accepting uncertainty changes fear in our mind into an adventure of its kind. For instance, when you are asked to experience paragliding or bungee jumping; you get tensed at that moment because you have not accepted it, which becomes your fear. But if you accept that, it becomes an adventure. When someone possesses something or achieves something, and if you don't accept it, that quickly turns into jealousy. But, on the other hand, your acceptance becomes your inspiration.

A small real-life example is: One day my daughter came to me weeping, saying that she scored lesser than her friend. I asked her, whether her friend was the topper of the class. Then she replied that many others scored more marks than her friend. I understood that she could not accept her friend getting higher marks, but she could accept others getting more marks than her. Similarly, when our siblings or some close relative or a friend is achieving something more significant, we cannot accept their growth; we get jealous. Even though there are many other people out there who are much more successful than us, we don't consider them as competitors.

This breaks down to a simple equation in life is a **situation + acceptance becomes a positive emotion, and a situation + non-acceptance becomes a negative emotion.**

This equation plays in all aspects of our lives for happiness, peace, emotional and qualitative life. Till date every time you get disturbed or experiencing mental stress, it is because of negative emotions caused due to non-acceptance of a situation, and it's the only thing that's keeping you from your peace. When you face any disturbance in life, keep asking yourself that "What am I not accepting to feel this kind of disturbance"?

The moment you accept the situation or the person, your negative emotion becomes positive. And always remember that the world is not in your control. It is your emotions that are in your possession. For example, we always think that the situation is making you angry, that person is making you angry, or that the person's action is making you angry. The reality is that your non-acceptance of the situation is making you angry.

CHAPTER II

Positive Attitude

"The mind is everything, what you think you become"

Buddha

Once, there was a guy who was in love with a girl. She was not the most beautiful and gorgeous but for him, she was everything. He used to dream about spending the rest of his life with her. His friends asked him, "why do you think so much about her? express your feelings and get to know if she likes you".

He felt that was the right way. The girl knew from the beginning that this guy loved her. One day when he proposed, she rejected him. His friends thought he would take alcohol and drugs and ruin his life. To their surprise, he was not depressed.

When they asked him why he was not sad, he replied, "why should Ifeel bad? I lost one who never loved me, and she lost the one who really loved andcared for her".

Positivity is about being optimistic about your thoughts, attitude, and actions. Positivity is maintaining your calmness, composure, hopefulness, enthusiasm, energy, and love for life. You perceive things differently when you have positive perspectives, making you more optimistic. You become a "good observer." You see only good in things, circumstances, events, and even accidents. Positivity helps you to look ahead regardless of your current situation. The first three steps to success, i.e., believe in yourself, set goals, and take action, are greatly influenced by positivity. The secret of success is focus, and positivity which helps you achieve whatever you want in life. When you are focused, you will achieve your goals. Positivity helps you to stay motivated during hard times.

The journey to success begins with a positive mindset. Positive thinking helps you to develop a growth mindset. You create a "can do" attitude only when you have positive thoughts. However, more than positive thoughts. you must also take action in the right direction with discipline.

Resilience is the key to success in life. Positivity affects your determination to never give up until you make it. Positivity helps to build your resilience. Optimism can improve your immunity, gives you better psychological and physical well-being.No matter how bad things are, you can always find something better. It lifts your spirit and your life.

I want to share a small story I heard on a spiritual talk show:

A rich man announced a big party and invited a lot of guests. At that party everyone was busy drinking, eating, dancing and enjoying the feast. Suddenly a small boy came and asked that rich man.... Uncle, may I know why you are so happy and hosting this party. His reply shocked everyone.

He explained that his new BMW car met with a bad accident, and the vehicle was completely damaged.

The boy couldn't restrict himself; he asked another question.... So, you arranged this party because your car was in an accident? The wealthiest man replied: I am not throwing the party because I lost my car in the accident, but I am throwing this party as the driver survived with just few scars. And also, he laughed and said **"I was the driver."**

In every negative situation, there will be a positive side. We should be optimistic enough to see the brighter side always.

In today's world, networking is essential for success. Successful people spend time building their networks. With a positive mindset, everyone around you can feel your positive vibration. They will see the positivity and always want to associate with you. People do not want to be around a negative person and a pessimist. Positive words have a heavy impact on human life.

Power of Positive words:

Using right word is a primary key to express our thoughts, emotions and beliefs. We can transform our lives by changing the use of words because our words reflect our thought process. If we consistently use hopeful and uplifting words, it influences our thoughts to bring hope and joy. By changing the phrases we think, speak, act, write, listen and read, we can create our ideal LIFESTYLE! Choose your words wisely and be the creator of your own life. You are the master of your ship, guiding it to safe lands of prosperity, abundance, happiness, and freedom.

DR. Emoto Masaru experimented that words have a vibration and will alter water molecules‘ structure. He found that uplifting, positive, and encouraging words created beautiful, balanced, and symmetric crystals in water molecules. On the other hand, destructive, hateful, and evil words had the opposite effect on the water molecules. The visual evidence is breathtaking. These experiments proved human thoughts and intentions can physically alter the molecular structure of anything in this universe.

Water from bottles labeled with cheerful massages had intricate structures and diamond-like reflectiveness when frozen and magnified. On the other hand, water labeled with negative words had collapsed structure.

Small intro about Dr. Emoto Masaru

Dr.Emoto Masaru was a Japanese businessman, author, and pseudoscientist who claimed that human consciousness could affect the molecular structure of water.His 2004 book The Hidden Messages in Water was a New York Times best seller. His conjecture evolved over the years. His early work revolved around pseudoscientific hypotheses that water could react to positive thoughts and words and that polluted water could be cleaned through prayer and positive visualization.

In 1999, Dr.Emoto published several volumes of a work entitled Messages from Water, containing photographs of ice crystals and accompanying experiments such as that of the ’rice in water‘ 30-day experiment.

Dr. Emoto claimed that water was a "blueprint for our reality" and that emotional "energies" and "vibrations" could change its physical structure. His water crystal experiments involved exposing water in glasses to different words, pictures, or music, then freezing it and examining the ice crystals' aesthetic properties with microscopic photography. He claimed that water exposed to positive speech and thoughts created visually "pleasing" ice crystals and that negative intentions yielded "ugly" ice formations.

Dr. Emoto held that different water sources produced other ice structures. For example, he had that water from a mountain stream, when frozen, showed structures of beautifully shaped geometric designs. Still, that water from polluted sources created distorted, randomly formed ice structures. He believed these changes could be eliminated by exposing water to ultraviolet light or electromagnetic waves. In 2008, Dr.Emoto published his findings in the Journal of Scientific Exploration, the Society for Scientific Exploration journal.

"Positive thought generates Positive feelings and attract Positive life experiences; sincere compliment is one of the most effective tools to teach and motivate others"

By ZIG Zaglar

Call of Action: Try to replace the negative words in to Positive words, if it's not possible replace with neutral word. For example: Problems should be changed to Opportunity or Challenges.

CHAPTER III

Gratitude

"Be thankful for what you have: you'll end up having more. If you concentrate on what you don't have, you will never ever have enough"

By Oprah Winfrey

Once upon a time, a king called his Minister and said, "I have so much money, wealth, and treasure, but I am not able to sleep well. I am not comfortable and I observe that the slaves outside my court, who do not even have money, sleep very well. Also, they live happily and remain cheerful. Why is there so much difference between them and me? They enjoy their life, whereas I am stressed".

The Minister says, your highness! You will understand this by secret formula 99.

The king asks, what is that?

The Minister calls the happy slave and asks the king to give him 100 gold coins. The Minister keeps cash inside his pocket secretly. The king gave the coins to the slave as a gift.

The slave was extremely happy and had never imagined receiving such a gift. He cheerfully went home and shared his joy with his wife and children. They were all very excited and, in a joyful mood, started counting the gold coins. To their surprise, there were only 99 gold coins. The children and the slave counted again and again and ended up with 99 cash only.

The wife then says, "you all do not know how to count. Let me count this time". When she counted, it was still 99 coins. Now she began to raise objections to the slave, saying, "You cannot keep anything safe. The king gave you 100 coins, but while coming home, you dropped one. Do you even know how much one gold coin is worth?

The slave replies no, saying he was very cautious. Next, the slave family searched the house for that 1 gold coin. In the morning, the slave goes to the king and the Minister with swollen eyes, sleepy, worried, and stressed.

The Minister then asks, "What happened to you? Why are you so sad?" The slave replies, "Your Highness! I made a mistake. You gave me 100 gold coins. I do not know where I dropped one on the way. The entire night my family spent searching for that coin. My family is very angry with me."

The Minister then took out that coin and said to him. "Here is your gold coin. Take this".

Now the point which the Minister told the king. I wish all of us would understand it and thus become stress-free. He said, Your highness! We all are facing the same problem as the slave. The slave had 99 gold coins and yet was not happy about that. Instead, he was sad and worried about the one coin he did not have. Similarly, we are unhappy about what we do not have in life, rather than being grateful and happy for what we have."

If we are not grateful for what we have, what makes us think we will be happy with more? Be grateful.

Gratitude exercise:

The more you count your blessings, the more blessings you receive in your life. So, keep journaling your blessings every day. Gratitude is nothing but being thankful for what we receive from people around us or being grateful for the giver. It creates a positive feeling about our life. It gives a sense of satisfaction.

Gratitude is a feeling of blessing for a lot of things like health, wealth, relationships, jobs, opportunities, and endless resources available to us. Although being thankful is one of the most straightforward, healthiest, and potent emotions, it is always much easier to focus on problems than blessings. But, paying attention to what we have and being thankful for having it, is the ultimate secret to a good life. By counting blessings daily, you condition your mind to look for the good in everything around you.

Life has its share of disappointments, frustration, losses, hurts, setbacks, and sadness. We go through each phase constantly comparing ourselves to others. Processing a life experience through gratefulness does not mean denying life's share of negativity. Instead, you begin to see the brighter side of life and feel better about it. It means using your power to transform an obstacle into an opportunity and reframing a loss into a potential gain.

It is easy to say thanks without being grateful but the key is expressing heartfelt Gratitude. Just imagine and reflect on how different your life would be without that particular thing or person. The moment this realization hits you, it transforms into strong feelings and emotions, and in this way, you can get into a powerful state of Gratitude.

No matter how bad things are, you can always find something to be grateful for, especially when you know that Gratitude will magically transform every negative situation into a positive one. It lifts your spirit and your life.

I want to share a small story I heard on a spiritual talk show:

Once a man named Ram was walking with his dog Tommy. While they were near the forest, a rabbit jumped before them, and Tommy, the dog, ran away after the rabbit. "Tommy was lost."

Ram searched for him for hours and then days. He notified all his neighbors and family members to help and put-up posters around the town, but each day ended with no success. He reimagined the incident; he thought about how horribly unlucky it was that the rabbit jumped out at the wrong time. *A week passed, and Tommy was brought back by a girl* named Vasanthi. Ram thanked her for bringing Tommy home, and then they had a casual chat. A few days later, they began to love each other and eventually became a couple. Now, Ram reimagined the incident that how lucky he was that his dog was lost and Vasanthi brought him back.

It was an excellent lucky day: *"Ram met with an accident."*

One day, Ram was driving to pick up Vasanthi and got into a car accident. He was quickly taken to the hospital after some tests and CT scans. The doctor informed him that he had a few scratches and nothing to worry about, but there was some piece of bad news and good news. The doctor saidRam got Tumor. Ram was shocked and angrily asked the doctor to explain how a tumor could be good news. The doctor explained. The bad news is you have a tumor in your brain. The good part is your tumor is in an early state where it can be removed with a bit of surgery. It is hard to notice such tumors until it is too late. "Your accident saved you."

Ram finally collected all the incidents of bad luck (losing his dog, getting in an accident) and all the great good fortune that came out of it (Meeting his love of life, discovering a curable tumor), demonstrating the incredibly random nature of luck.

Moral of the story:

It is impossible to tell whether anything that happens is good or bad because you never know what the consequences of the misfortune will be or the effects of good fortune.

Be grateful, and show your Gratitude even for your misfortune.

"When life is sweet, Say Thank You and celebrate.
When life is bitter, say thank you and grow"

Call of Action: As soon as you wake up start your day with 10 random gratitude sentences every day. Start showing Gratitude towards life by journaling daily and penning down 10 sentences, which randomly includes all areas of your life like

CHAPTER IV

Self-Love:

"Don't forget to say "I Love you" to the dearest person in the world"

If we want to improve relationships, it starts from self. Everyone needs love on this planet. Love includes acceptance, care, compassion, appreciation, belief, trust, forgiveness, and happiness. Hence self-love means nothing but self-acceptance, self-care, self-forgiveness, and self-satisfaction. In life, we need to concentrate on what we can change but need to accept what we can't. For example, we can't change our features eyes, nose, ears, face, height, color, etc. To groom ourselves is in our hands, health and fitness are in our hands, and dressing well is in our hands. However, we always focus on what we can't change, what we don't have. It criticizes us, makes us complain about ourselves, and abuse fate. It creates dissatisfaction in our life. Self-love changes the entire outlook of one's life. So, practice self-love.

Before a person can practice it, we first need to understand what it means.

Self-love is a state of appreciation for oneself that grows from actions that support our physical, psychological, and spiritual growth. Self-love means having a high regard for our own well-being and happiness. Self-love means taking care of our needs and not sacrificing our well-being to please others. Finally, self-love means not settling for less than we deserve. Self-love can mean something different to each person because we all have many different ways to take care of ourselves. Therefore, figuring out what self-love looks like for you as an individual is an integral part of your mental health.

What does self-love mean to you? Talking to and about yourself with love Prioritizing yourself, giving yourself a break from self-judgment, trusting yourself, being true to yourself, being nice to yourself, setting healthy boundaries, forgiving yourself when you aren't being genuine or friendly to yourself.

For many people, self-love is another way to say self-care. To practice self-care, we often need to go back to the basics and

- Listen to our bodies.
- Take breaks from work and move/stretch.
- Put the phone down, connect to yourself or do something creative.
- Eating healthily, but sometimes indulging in your favorite foods.

Self-love means accepting yourself and everything you are, accepting your emotions, and putting your physical, emotional, and mental well-being first.

How and Why to Practice Self Love:

So now we know that self-love motivates you to make healthy choices in life. When you hold yourself in high esteem, you're more likely to choose things that nurture your well-being and serve you well. These things may be in the form of eating healthy, exercising, or having healthy relationships.

Ways to practice self-love include:

a. Becoming mindful: People with more self-love tend to know what they think, feel, and want.
b. Taking actions based on need rather than want: By staying focused on what you need, you turn away from automatic behavioral patterns that get you into trouble, keep you stuck in the past, and lessen self-love.
c. Practicing good self-care: You will love yourself more when you take better care of your basic needs. People high in self-love nourish themselves daily through healthy activities, like sound nutrition, exercise, proper sleep, intimacy, and healthy social

interactions.

d. Making room for healthy habits: Start truly caring for yourself by mirroring that in what you eat, how you exercise and what you love doing the most. Do stuff, not to "get it done" or because you "have to," but because you care about yourself.

Finally, to practice self-love, start by being kind, patient, gentle, and compassionate to yourself, the way you would with someone you care about.

"You yourself, as much as anybody in the entire universe deserve your love and affection"

By SHARON SALZBERG

Call of Action: Mirror exercise twice a day saying I am whole; I am complete and I am perfect the way I am right now. I love my self the way I am.

CHAPTER V

Complement

"Sincere compliments cost nothing and can accomplish so much. In any relationship they are applause that refreshes"

By Steve Goodier

Once in a factory, there were many workers. Among them was John, who was known as the factory's most sincere and hardworking employee. He has excellent repot with everyone, respects everyone, and has good relations with the company management.

The factory shifts start at 10 AM and ends at 6 PM. The watchman at the gate used to keep watch at the entrance, and when the workers went away, he would close the factory by locking the gate.

It was Monday, and John was busy doing his task; at 6 PM, all the workers finished their work and went home, but he was so involved in the work that he overlooked time. He was busy with work even past 8 PM. As the watchman noticed that John did not leave work, he went into John's cabin to ask why he was still working at a late hour. John was shocked and said," How do you come to know that I'm still working as my cabin is far away from the gate?"

The watchman said politely," You are the only employee to greet me good morning while coming in and good night while departing. Today, I missed a good night from you. I guessed that you may still be working."

Moral:

Your compliments always help strengthen your relations with others, don't hesitate to compliment others. They cost nothing.

Example: Your haircut looks great.

Your speech was so motivating.

You are a perfect friend.

I can't tell you how great it was talking to you last week when I was upset.

Feeling valued and appreciated are basic human needs. Psychotherapist in California and author of the book "***Marriage Meetings for Lasting Love: 30 Minutes a Week to the Relationship You've Always Wanted***" mentioned that appreciation is also foundational in relationships with our partners, spouses, and friends. It's part of what makes us want to cooperate and collaborate with those around us. And if you come across a challenge, knowing that you're appreciated helps you want to work through and overcome that challenge. Compliments help us communicate the appreciation we feel toward one another. So, I would define a compliment as any sort of sincere appreciation of a trait in someone or a behavior or an appearance. And that makes us feel good.

Scientists have found that receiving a compliment light up the parts of your brain that get activated when you get paid a monetary reward. Other research (from the same group of researchers) suggests compliments and praise may help us learn new motor skills and behaviors.

Being in the habit of giving compliments helps us notice and appreciate what's good and what we like in those around us. Compliments also help us like one another. Behaviors that get rewarded are likely to be repeated. So, if you tell someone how much you like that they smiled at you when you greeted each other, they will likely smile again on seeing you. Giving someone a compliment can also be a good conversation starter, or an excellent way to get over an awkward bump in a conversation whether it's a conversation with someone you know or have just met.In this way and others, it's not just the receiver who walks away better off. Compliments benefit the giver, too. "So being complimentary helps us create an optimistic, happier outlook." *We should know how to give good compliments.*

Compliments should be sincere:

It might seem harmless to tell someone that their shoes are pretty, even though you think they're hideous. But most of the time, the genuine compliment will go farther than the insincere one.

So much of what we say gets communicated by what your voice tone is implied, and your body language. Most of us have a sixth sense when sniffing out people who pretend to give compliments. Everybody has qualities that deserve complimenting.

Pay attention:

The key to giving compliments (and being good at giving compliments) is paying attention to the people around you and the details. "Notice what you like or appreciate about the person."

Be specific:

The best compliments are specific. They refer to character traits, behaviors, or appearance. (Yes, we all tend to like to know that we're viewed as attractive) Hearing that someone thinks you're thoughtful, kind, or pretty is nice, but those compliments apply to many people. Calling something specific shows the other person you're interested in and paying attention.

Rather than just telling someone they look nice, say to that person: "You look so handsome in that blue shirt you're wearing. It matches your eyes."

When it comes to giving compliments, make it rain:

Ideally, we give and receive compliments daily in our close relationships. However, it's effortless to take one another for granted or only mention the negative things that need solutions. So, making a concerted effort to notice all the good things about your partner (or family member or friend) is essential.

If you get in the habit of giving compliments frequently, you'll notice what's going well, which can help strengthen any relationship.

Receive compliments with grace:

Sometimes people feel uncomfortable receiving compliments because they were taught (or might think) that accepting them equates to bragging or boosting, But it's not. Instead, compliments are about communicating what you appreciate and what's working with those around you.

Learning how to graciously accept compliments is just as important as learning how to give them. After all, denying a compliment is another way of telling someone they're wrong or that their opinion or perspective is wrong (which is kind of rude if you think about it). "It's like refusing to accept a gift from someone,"

When in doubt, a simple "thank you" works.

A small theory how complimenting works at work place; Establishing a positive organizational culture in which employees and managers support one another should be a top priority for organizations. Expressing praise and gratitude is particularly important for keeping up morale. Gratitude makes people feel valued, and positive feedback has been shown to mitigate the negative effects of stress on employee performance.

Neuroscientists have even shown that the brain processes verbal affirmations similarly to financial rewards. The former CEO of Ford has been quoted a saying for his employees, "It's all about appreciating, respecting, and thanking them at every step of the way." While the importance of expressing praise and gratitude for establishing a positive organizational culture is evident, our research suggests that people may not compliment because they underestimate the positive impact of kind words on others.

These experiments highlight a critical psychological barrier to creating more positive organizational cultures:

When deciding whether to express praise or appreciation to another person, doubt creeps in. We find that people are overly concerned about their ability to convey compliments skillfully ("What if my delivery is awkward?"), and their anxiety leaves them excessively pessimistic about their messages‘ effects. Sadly, people's pessimism causes them to refrain from engaging in this behavior that would make everyone better off.

Research shows that people also underestimate how much recipients appreciate gratitude. In one study, participants wrote gratitude letters expressing their appreciation to someone. The recipients of these letters were then asked how they felt receiving them. When the researchers compared recipients' feelings to senders' expectations, they found that senders underestimated how positive recipients would feel and overestimated how awkward they would feel. Here again, people's overly pessimistic beliefs can prevent them from doing others an act of kindness that would increase their feelings of appreciation.

There is ample evidence that giving someone else a boost, whether giving compliments or expressing gratitude, has a mood-lifting effect and contributes to well-being. This means that everyone benefits, both givers and receivers alike. Creating a positive organizational culture is important, perhaps now more than ever. But we often hold back unnecessarily because we aren't well calibrated to the actual effects our positive messages have on others.

"Gratitude is not about a one-time holiday party, day off, or spot bonus...It is about creating a *culture*of gratitude." Of course, creating such a culture is more important now than ever. But to get there, we must recognize the value of regularly expressing appreciation to one another and what a positive impact such gestures can have.

"Positive thought generates Positive feelings and attract Positive life experiences; sincere compliment is one of the most effective tools to teach and motivate others"

By ZIG Zaglar

Call of Action: Before going to bed check your self, whether you complimented or appreciated minimum 3 people or not, consciously do an effort to compliment others or their work.

CHAPTER VI

Forgiveness

"Forgive others, not because they deserve forgiveness, but because you deserve peace"

By Mel Ribbin

Forgiveness is the best medicine to heal the pain in any relation by letting out grudges and bitterness. When someone you care about hurts you, you can hold on to anger, resentment, and thoughts of revenge or embrace forgiveness and move forward. Who hasn't been hurt by the actions or words of another? Perhaps a parent constantly criticized you growing up, a colleague sabotaged a project, or your partner had an affair. Or maybe you've had a traumatic experience, such as being physically or emotionally abused by someone close to you. These wounds can leave you with lasting feelings of anger and bitterness, even vengeance. But if you don't practice forgiveness, you might be the one who pays most dearly. By embracing forgiveness, you can also embrace peace, hope, gratitude, and joy. Consider how forgiveness can lead you down the path of physical, emotional, and spiritual well-being.

Before explaining forgiveness, I would like to introduce a person who healed her cancer by practicing forgiveness. Popularly known as Louise Hay.

Hay stated in an interview that she was born in Los Angeles to a poor mother who remarried Louise's violent stepfather, Ernest Carl Wanzenreid (1903–1992), who physically abused her and her mother. When she was about 5, she was raped by a neighbor. At 15, she dropped out of University High School in Los Angeles without a diploma, became pregnant, and gave up her newborn baby girl for adoption on her 16th birthday. She then moved to Chicago, where she worked in low-paying jobs. In 1950, she moved again to New

York. At this point, she changed her first name and began a career as a fashion model. She achieved success. In 1954, she married the English businessman Andrew Hay (1928–2001); after 14 years of marriage, she felt devastated when he left her for another woman, Sharman Douglas (1928–1996). Hay said she founded the First Church of Religious Science on 48th Street, which taught her the transformative power of thought. Hay revealed that she studied the New Thought works of authors such as Florence Scovel Shinn, who believed that positive thinking could change people's material circumstances. In addition, religious Science founder Ernest Holmes taught that positive thinking could heal the body.

In the early 1970s, she became a Religious Science practitioner. In this role, she led people in spoken affirmations, which she believed would cure their illnesses, and became famous as a workshop leader. She also recalled how she had studied Transcendental Meditation with the Maharishi Mahesh Yogi at the Maharishi International University in Fairfield, Iowa. Hay described how in 1977 or 1978, she was diagnosed with "incurable" cervical cancer. She concluded that holding on to her resentment for her childhood abuse and rape contributed to its onset. She reported how she had refused conventional medical treatment and began a regime of forgiveness, coupled with therapy, nutrition, reflexology, and occasional colonic enemas. She claimed in the interview that she got rid of cancer by this method but, while swearing to its truth, admitted that she had outlived every doctor who could confirm this story.

In 1976, Hay wrote and self-published her first book, *Heal Your Body*, which began as a small pamphlet containing a list of different bodily ailments and their "probable" metaphysical causes. This pamphlet was later enlarged and extended into her book *You Can Heal Your Life*, published in 1984. In February 2008, it was fourth on the New York Times paperback advice bestsellers list. Hay died in her sleep on August 30, 2017, at age 90.

What is forgiveness?

Forgiveness means different things to different people. Generally, however, it involves a decision to let go of resentment and thoughts of revenge. The act that hurt or an act of offend might always be with you, but forgiveness can lessen its grip on you and help free you from the control of the person who harmed you. In addition, forgiveness can also lead to feelings of understanding, empathy, and compassion for the one who hurt you. Forgiveness doesn't mean forgetting or excusing the harm done to you or making up with the person who caused the damage. Instead, forgiveness brings a kind of peace that helps you go on with your life.Being hurt by someone you love and trust can cause anger, sadness, and confusion. Grudges filled with resentment, vengeance, and hostility can take root if you dwell on hurtful events or situations. If you allow negative feelings to crowd out positive feelings, you might find yourself swallowed up by your own bitterness or sense of injustice. Of course, some people are naturally more forgiving than others, but when you hold grudges, you will be the person who suffers the most.

Letting go of grudges and bitterness can improve health and peace of mind. Forgiveness can lead to healthier relationships, improved mental health, less anxiety, stress, and hostility, lower blood pressure, fewer symptoms of depression, a more robust immune system, improved heart health, and improved self-esteem.

When I was delivering training about forgiveness, a few of the audience asked me how they could reach that state of forgiveness?

Forgiveness is a commitment to a personalized process of change. To move away from suffering is to forgive. You might recognize the value of forgiveness and how it can improve your life. Identify what needs healing and who needs to be forgiven. Acknowledge your emotions about the harm done to you and how they affect your behavior, and work to release them. Choose to forgive the person who offended you. Move away from your role as victim and release the control and power the offending person and situation have had in your life.

As you let go of grudges, you'll no longer define your life by how you've been hurt. You might even find compassion and understanding.

If you find yourself stuck:

Practice empathy. Try seeing the situation from the other person's point of view.

Ask yourself why he or she would behave in such a way, and you might have also reacted similarly if you faced the same situation.

Reflect on times you've hurt others and those who've forgiven you.

Write in a journal, pray or use guided meditation — or talk with a person you've found to be wise and compassionate, such as a spiritual leader, a mental health provider, or an impartial loved one or friend.

Be aware that forgiveness is a process; even the smallest of hurts may need to be revisited and forgiven repeatedly. With this, we get a question in mind "what if the person I'm forgiving doesn't change"?

Getting another person to change his or her actions, behavior, or words isn't the point of forgiveness. Think of forgiveness more about how it can change your life — by bringing you peace, happiness, and emotional and spiritual healing. Forgiveness can take away the power the other person continues to wield in your life.

If you are the one who needs forgiveness,

The first step is to assess and acknowledge the wrongs you've done and how they have affected others. Also, avoid judging yourself too harshly.

If you're genuinely sorry for something you've said or done, consider admitting it to those you've harmed. Speak of your sincere sorrow or regret, and ask for forgiveness — without making excuses.

Remember, however, you can't force someone to forgive you. Others need to move to forgiveness in their own time. Whatever happens, commit to treating others with compassion, empathy, and respect. However, there is no guarantee.

Forgiveness could lead to reconciliation if the hurtful event involved someone whose relationship you otherwise value. This is only sometimes the case, however.

Reconciliation might be impossible if the offender has died or is unwilling to communicate with you. In other cases, reconciliation might not be appropriate. Still, forgiveness is possible — even if reconciliation isn't.

"You don't forgive people because you're weak. You forgive them because you're strong enough to know that people make mistakes"

Call of Action: If you have deep disturbed thoughts and not able to clear it out "SIT WITH YOURSELF" and recall who made you feel bad, resented, angry, frustrated and any other kind of negative emotions which you have experienced since your childhood. Takeout every name and write it on a paper, forgive them from deep within, you just imagine they are Infront of you and smile at them, show the love and compassionate eye on them, then burn the paper and blow the ashes. Take a deep breath. Test yourself after few days if you remember the situation, if you're heart beat is normal and do not feel any kind of sadness or anger, it means you forgot the situation and forgave them completely. If not, you have to do the same exercise again and again till you release the negative feeling

CHAPTER VII

Happiness

"Happiness is not something readymade. It comes from your own actions"

Dalai Lama

Happiness depends on our satisfaction in different areas of life. If our health is not good, we can't be happy. Facing financial challenges and issues in our job, business, or profession will not make us happy either. However, we are not satisfied because of the wrong choices we make. But most times, the reason for not being happy is relationship issues. In our life, few relations are chosen by us; some turn unhappy due to bad decisions. But few relations are given to us by birth in which we do not have any say, like our parents, siblings, offspring, and other blood relations. Therefore, we need to accept and never ever question God's decision. If we accept and understand everyone is unique and has different mentalities, happiness and satisfaction are all about accepting this fact and cherishing every moment with people instead of expecting others being bound to satisfy our unrealistic expectations.

Life is short. Yet, it's an established scientific fact that happy people tend to live longer. Your choices can help you feel great, reduce stress, and be more content. So, now's the time to boost your happiness by making happy choices!

Happiness shouldn't be determined by what happens to us on a daily bases but also by the choices we make. Making happier choices is a liberating way to live. It helps us understand that happiness is something we can all learn to control. It is easy to create positive emotions by making simple choices, such as being more kind to yourself. Also, you can empower your happiness by becoming more self-reliant.

What if I told you there is a powerful chemical factory inside your head, and you hold the keys to these happy 'drugs'? You can give yourself a moderate and healthy DOSE anytime you need to, without external drugs. This is unlocked by doing simple actions to release them?

D.O.S.E means the natural production of 'feel-good' brain chemicals such as: --

Dopamine (responsible for intense pleasure.) Dopamine is most notably involved in helping us feel pleasure as part of the brain's reward system. For example, shopping, smelling cookies baking in the oven, and having your favorite food trigger dopamine release or a "dopamine rush." This feel-good neurotransmitter is also involved in reinforcement.

Oxytocin (known as the love hormone.) Oxytocin is released in response to the activation of sensory nerves during labor, breastfeeding, and sexual activity. In addition, oxytocin is released in response to low-intensity stimulation of the skin, e.g., in response to touch, hug, stroking, warmth... etc.

Serotonin (a natural mood enhancer.) when we pedal a bicycle or lift weights, our body releases more tryptophan, the amino acid your brain uses to make serotonin. This boost in serotonin (along with other endorphins and other neurotransmitters) is why many people get that feeling of euphoria known as a "runner's high" after an intense workout.

Endorphins (natural pain-killer) are released during pleasurable activities such as exercise, massage, eating, and sex. Other activities like helping others, social service, achieving something, appreciation, and receiving compliments can also release a combination of dopamine, oxytocin, and serotonin.

It's always a choice to consider these natural alternatives for the artificial stimulants we use. No one else has the keys but you - and it's legal too. So, unlock your inner doors of joy by making happy choices today.

How we perceive ourselves and the natural world around us depends greatly on our beliefs. Our beliefs are at the roots of our happiness or unhappiness. We may have a free mind space for a better life if we change them. We can break free from a mind-made prison by changing our inner beliefs. We all have fantastic potentiality deep inside us, waiting to break through, but our minds often hinder us. All we need to do is change our interpretations of life, as interpretations are just meanings we self-create within our minds - 'meanings' that hold us back from personal freedom.

For example, instead of a core belief like 'I will be free when I am rich' – a detrimental interpretation to our present sense of happiness – why not choose a more empowering idea such as 'I am free because I control my mind?' When people believe they have no control over their life situation, they begin to behave helplessly. A mental state called 'learned helplessness' arises from years and years of limiting beliefs. This is an established behavioral theory to describe people with negative expectations that their life is out of control, leading to a total inability to act effectively.

You can choose your destiny. You can be your own boss. This brave new world means unique opportunities for ordinary people who want to break free from the rat race and choose an empowering reality. Everything has changed with our latest technology. Barriers to market entry are crumbling into dust. Now is a great time to embrace personal freedom. However, you may need a reality check if you still have any lingering doubts. --Are your thoughts holding you back from living the life of your dreams? --Have other people's views and opinions trapped you with a set of limiting beliefs? --Do you choose to see yourself more as a 'character' in a story rather than the author of your life? We should be more like authors. In other words, we shouldn't allow ourselves to lose control of events in our lives. Instead, we should make significant changes if we wish so. Take ownership. Take charge. Write our own destinies.

Call of Action: Do whatever makes you feel happy, minimum10 to 30 minutes a day or a lot few hours in a week to pamper your soul. For example, singing, dancing, cooking, gardening, playing with kids, playing with pets, chat with old friend or childhood friend, visiting old age homes, helping strangers and see the smile on their face, write a letter to your loved one.... etc.

CHAPTER VIII

Physical Health

"Your body is your most priceless possession take care of it"

Jack Lalane

Before discussing physical health, I would like to tell you how I realized the importance of health. My mother had a heart attack at the age of 40 and I became more health conscious from then. I wonder how her health was spoiled. She suffered from various lifestyle deceases like blood pressure, diabetes, and asthma. She never used to eat outside and never had any junk food. Her first medication started in her early 40s for blood pressure, and other health complications were added as she aged year by year. She was prescribed 20 tablets per day and high-dose insulin injections twice a day for so many years. Nebulization and by-pap were also included in her daily routine. I have literally seen what living death means. No medicine cured her; she only extended her life with multiple complications. When I worked in the healthcare industry, I understood one thing after attending many pieces of training, health care is different from medical care.

My mother has taken medical care, not health care. I realized that the chemicals she consumed worked on one issue and indirectly affecting other organs. Her lifestyle has slowly and gradually developed multiple complications. I never saw her diabetes under control, and slowly her dosage got increased to control her insulin levels. Finally, I understood the real meaning of this powerful statement. "Prevention is better than cure." "Health is wealth." "If we don't take food as medicine, we should take medicine as food."

We should have basic knowledge of the human body and its structure. Our physical body comprises 5 elements, Earth, Sky,

Water, Fire, and Air; these elements play a significant role in our physical well-being.

Element of Air

Represents oxygen which we take through breathing day in and day out. It is the primary element. We can't live without breathing. Let me explain the science behind this. Oxygen is all around us in the Air we breathe, which is a good thing because we cannot live without it. Oxygen is so vital that it will lead us to death if deprived of it for only a short time. Why do we need oxygen, and how do our bodies acquire it? Let's take a look.

Oxygen fuels our cells and helps provide the basic building blocks our bodies need to survive. Our cells combine oxygen with nitrogen and hydrogen to produce various proteins that build new cells. When oxygen is combined with carbon and hydrogen, you get carbohydrates that provide energy to our bodies that are necessary for us to live. Oxygen is also required for constructing replacement cells for our bodies. Every day, about seven hundred billion cells in our bodies wear out and must be replaced. Without oxygen, our bodies cannot build these new cells.

Oxygen is also an essential part of our immune system. It is used to help kill bacteria and fuel the cells that make up our body's defenses against viruses and other invaders. Air that has passed through UV air sanitizers is perfect for our body's immune system, as it has been cleansed of bacteria and other agents before it enters our respiratory systems. This makes it easier for the body to access oxygen and keeps it from receiving a fresh influx of germs and particulate matter that comes into the body through contaminated air that has not been sanitized.

Finally, it is essential to note that the human eye needs oxygen to function well. However, the eye receives oxygen in a manner that is unique from the rest of the body. Few blood vessels travel to the eye, so our eyes absorb much of the oxygen they need directly through the cornea. The cornea is built in such a way as to diffuse oxygen directly into the body from the air. If the air has traveled through (air purifiers) first, it can enter the eye without causing irritation.

It is through the human body's respiratory system that the cells receive the oxygen they need to properly function. The entry "gates" of the respiratory system are the mouth and nose. This is where the air comes into the human body, and this air is then directed toward and down the trachea into the lungs.

The body works best when air is relatively pure before it is inhaled. That is why many people use (air purifiers) at work and at home. These purifiers remove particulate matter, such as dust and smoke, from the air, making it easier for the respiratory system to do its job. (Room ionizers) work in a similar fashion to remove this matter from the air. Essentially, they attract the stuff we should not inhale, pulling it out of the air and attaching it to a filter that can later be cleaned.

Once air enters the lungs through the trachea and bronchial tubes, it is directed to tiny sacs called alveoli. There are more than six hundred million alveoli in an adult's lung; in these alveoli, oxygen passes from the air into the bloodstream. In respiration, carbon dioxide passes from the bloodstream into the alveoli. It is eventually directed out of the human body through the bronchial tubes to the trachea to the nose and mouth, where this air is exhaled. The human circulatory system then takes the oxygen throughout the body and brings carbon dioxide back to the lungs. The entire process is repeated with every breath that human beings take.

Practice the ancient technique of Pranayama, regularly, Sudarshan kriya, or any breathing exercise.

Element of Water

Water is also an essential element for our human body. Having adequate water in your body is critical to nearly every part. Not only will maintaining your recommended daily intake help you to keep your current state of good health, but it could also improve it in the long run. The amount of water you need will depend on your environment and climate, how physically active you are, and whether you are suffering from an illness, ailment, or other health problems.

Here are some ways to make sure that you drink enough water:

Carry a water bottle with you wherever you go. Keep taking sips from it as and when you feel the need. Track your water intake. Make sure you consume the optimum amount every day, which is a minimum of half your body weight in ounces/milligrams

All plants and animals need water to survive. There can be no life on earth without water. Why is water so important? Because 60 percent of our body weight is made up of water. Our bodies use water in all the cells, organs, and tissues to help regulate body temperature and maintain other bodily functions. Because our bodies lose water through breathing, sweating, and digestion, it's crucial to rehydrate and replace water by drinking fluids and eating foods that contain water.

Let's look at all the ways water impacts our lives...

Water helps by creating saliva:

Water is the main component of saliva. It is critical for breaking down solid food and keeping your mouth healthy. If you find your mouth is drier than usual, increase your water intake. If that does not work, consult your doctor.

Water regulates body temperature:

Staying hydrated is critical to maintaining an average body temperature. Our bodies lose water when we sweat and in hot environments. Sweat keeps our bodies cool, but our body temperatures will increase if we do not replenish the necessary water content. That lack of water causes dehydration, which in turn causes levels of electrolytes and plasma to drop.

Water aids cognitive functions:

Proper hydration is crucial to staying in good cognitive shape. Research has shown that inadequate water intake can negatively impact our focus, alertness, and short-term memory.

Water protects the tissues, spinal cord, and joints:

Water helps lubricate and cushion our joints, spinal cord, and tissues. This helps us to be more physically active and reduces the discomfort caused by conditions such as arthritis.

Water helps excrete the waste in our bodies through perspiration, urination, and defecation:

Our bodies use water to sweat, urinate, and pass healthy bowel movements. We all need water to replenish fluids lost from sweating. We also need water in our systems to have healthy stools and avoid constipation. Drinking enough water helps our kidneys to work more efficiently, thus preventing kidney stones.

Water maximizes our physical performance:

Drinking plenty of water while working out, participating in sports, or just being on the move, is essential. Keeping ourselves hydrated also affects our strength, power, and endurance.

Water helps to boost our energy levels:

Drinking water helps to boost our metabolic rate. This boost has a positive impact on our energy levels. One study has found that drinking 500 milliliters of water can increase the metabolic rate by 30 percent in both men and women. The adverse effects of exercising in the heat without staying hydrated can result in serious medical incidents. In fact, extreme dehydration can cause seizures and, sometimes, even death.

Water prevents overall dehydration:

Dehydration is the result of the body being deprived of adequate water. And, since water is critical for the successful functioning of many bodily functions, dehydration can be very dangerous. Even leading to fatal consequences. Severe dehydration can lead to serious outcomes, including swelling in the brain, kidney failure and seizures.

Element of FIRE (SUN)

From promoting the growth of plants and crops to keeping people warm, sunlight is essential for life. In addition, many people enjoy the feeling of the sun, and there is increasing evidence to support its many health benefits. Sunlight Soak 60% of your body in daylight in the morning, ideally for 20 minutes or more. The healthy function of your circadian rhythm needs to give you energy and improve your sleep. Vitamin D is also vital and much better than taking a supplement. I like to combine sun-soaking with other things by going outside or doing my morning exercises out in the sun. However, widespread awareness that too much exposure to UV radiation from the sun can cause skin cancer has prompted people to be cautious about spending time in the sun.

However, just as people need to protect themselves from too much sun, they should also ensure they get enough to enjoy the health benefits of sunlight. Finding the right balance can help people maintain optimal levels of vitamin D and enjoy the mental health benefits of a sunny day without placing themselves at risk. The various health benefits of sunlight. It initiating the process of producing vitamin D in the body may be the best known. When UVB rays hit human skin, they interact with the 7-DHC protein to produce vitamin D3. People can get vitamin D from their diet and supplements, but sunlight is an important source of this essential nutrient. Vitamin D is necessary for vital biological processes to take place in the body. It benefits in numerous ways supporting healthy bones, managing calcium levels reducing inflammation, and supporting the immune system and glucose metabolism. Researchers have noted a link between exposure to the sun and lower blood pressure levels, with reduced death rates from cardiovascular issues. They suggest that exposure to sunlight triggers the skin to release stores of nitrogen oxides, which cause arteries to dilate, lowering blood pressure and may reduce the impact of metabolic syndrome. According to other research, increased sun exposure may protect people from diseases like type 1 diabetes, multiple sclerosis (MS), several forms of cancer, including colon, breast, and prostate cancer, and non-Hodgkin lymphoma.

Sunlight also supports better sleep and sets people's circadian rhythms by regulating serotonin and melatonin levels.

Being in the sun generally makes people feel good, and many scientific reasons exist for this effect.

One of these is that exposure to UVB rays causes human skin to produce beta-endorphins, hormones that reduce pain. Their other benefits include the following:

Promoting a sensation of well-being and improving mood, boosting the immune system, relieving pain, promoting relaxation, helping wounds heal, helping people feel more alert, and reducing depression.

Element of Sky

It is the unending (Ananth) regions remote from the Earth, in which not only our solar system but the entire galaxy exists. Its effective forces are light, heat, gravitational force, waves and magnetic field.

Aakash or Space is infinite and limitless. It is related to our sense of hearing in a structure, the space element is related to the center position or the Brahmasthan. It is the source of cosmic radiation or cosmic energy. The sky element means cosmic energy. It is important that the Brahmasthan be kept open, clean and light.

So, the actual underlined meaning for fasting is to cleanse out our center position to keep it clean and open. The fire created is an energy produced by the human body while fasting is vital.

Here are 8 health benefits of fasting — backed by science:

1. Promotes Blood Sugar Control by Reducing Insulin Resistance
2. Promotes Better Health by Fighting Inflammation
3. May Enhance Heart Health by Improving Blood Pressure, Triglycerides and Cholesterol Levels
4. May Boost Brain Function and Prevent Neurodegenerative Disorders

5. Aids Weight Loss by Limiting Calorie Intake and Boosting Metabolism
6. Increases Growth Hormone Secretion, Which Is Vital for Growth, Metabolism, Weight Loss and Muscle Strength
7. Could Delay Aging and Extend Longevity
8. May Aid in Cancer Prevention and Increase the Effectiveness of Chemotherapy

How to Start Fasting

There are many different types of fasts, making it easy to find a method that fits your lifestyle.

Here are a few of the most common types of fasting:

- **Water fasting:** Involves drinking only water for a set amount of time.
- **Juice fasting:** Entails only drinking vegetable or fruit juice for a certain period.
- **Intermittent fasting:** Intake is partially or completely restricted for a few hours up to a few days at a time and a normal diet is resumed on other days.
- **Partial fasting:** Certain foods or drinks such as processed foods, animal products or caffeine are eliminated from the diet for a set period.
- **Calorie restriction:** Calories are restricted for a few days every week.

Within these categories are also more specific types of fasts.

For example, intermittent fasting can be broken down into subcategories, such as alternate-day fasting, which involves eating every other day, or time-restricted feeding, which entails limiting intake to just a few hours each day.

To get started, try experimenting with different types of fasting to find what works best for you.

Element of Earth

Our physical self combines earth, water, air, fire, and akasha. Earth is the most basic and stable of the five elements. Regarding the energy system and chakras, the earth element is associated with the Muladhara. It is the basis that all the other elements are built. Though the elements of the earth are part of the physical matter around us, we should start to perceive and understand it from the basis of our lives because most people only experience their bodies and minds. Knowing and experiencing the element of earth from within is part of the Yogic process.

Whenever you eat food, you swallow a part of the earth. Essentially, we take part of the planet to sustain the body. There is a deep understanding in Indian culture that the world is the mother. We are born on the earth. Our biological mother is only a representative who is also born on the same earth. The real mother is the soil that we carry as our bodies. The body you take now has been millions of bodies in the past – insects, snakes, cows, monkeys, and human beings. I am not talking about the evolutionary process, but the soil goes through every form of life. Soil is not a commodity. It is older, wiser, and far more intelligent and capable than you. It is a far more extensive process than you are as a person. Here I want to explain how nature and mother earth gives energy to humankind in the form of food containing different kinds of minerals, vitamins, and other essential nutrients.

Earth, as we discussed under the health area, I am going to discuss plant-based healthy food, as we all belong to mother earth.

Because unhealthy food habits not only degrade your physical wellness but also your mental fitness. Often, we are only concerned about pleasing our taste buds and not caring about our health. But unfortunately, the unhealthy and convenient food we consume daily to cut down cooking time and effort from our busy schedule poses an unimaginable threat to our bodies. That is why I want to discuss the importance of healthy food. It may be difficult for you to switch to a healthy diet after consuming unhealthy food for a long time, but with some patience and effort, you will get used to it and eventually lead a healthy life. Plant-based foods benefit us by making our bodies healthy and fit.

Healthy eating does not mean having only boiled meals, eating less, or saying no to fat. **Instead, healthy food habits involve switching to a well-balanced, nutritious diet, i.e., eating everything in the right amount, at the right time, and with the right combination.** Don't wholly exclude fats or overdo the fibers and proteins! Also, remember that children should be given a mix and match of all types of food because this is the age for physical and mental development.

Here are reasons why eating healthy is essential:

What we eat provides all the essential nutrients to our bodies. This supplies our body with the right energy to do our daily work. And all these nutrients come only from healthy food, not anything and everything we eat.

Healthy food is needed to stimulate growth hormones that gradually increase our height with age.

Healthy food is also needed for the functioning of our system. All the nutrients from healthy food trigger body and brain cells to actively run and perform their task.

Healthy food improves the immune system, preventing you from falling sick quickly. A strong immunity fights against all disease-causing bacteria and viruses.It is generally advised to cut out fat from our diet. However, this is often mistaken as entirely excluding even healthy fats. The unhealthy fats that should not be eaten are saturated and trans-fat. Monounsaturated fats, polyunsaturated fats, omega 3, and omega 6 fatty acids are essential for our health, just like proteins and vitamins. These fats get stored under skin cells, transforming into energy required for physical and mental activities. Therefore, we must include these in our daily diet.

Healthy food can help you maintain a well-shaped body without falling into the evil trap of weight gain or obesity.

Eating a balanced diet gives us all the necessary nutrients for healthy living. These include macronutrients like proteins, carbohydrates, fats, vitamins, minerals, water, and fiber.

Proteins: An essential nutrient that should be included in our daily diet

- Proteins are needed to build up new tissues and renew old tissues.
- It protects the muscles, which are non-fat tissue mass.
- Proteins are also needed to produce enzymes and hormones that control the various functions of our body.

People on a diet often end up avoiding protein intake in their diet. **This is not very healthy as it may weaken the muscles, making them prone to injury.**

Carbohydrates: The ultimate energy sources for your body, carbohydrates are the power suppliers to your body

- Energy is needed in large quantities in adolescents and adults.
- It is essential for your growth and development to increase the metabolic rate and helps you remain active throughout the day.
- Intake of sufficient amounts of carbohydrates in food prevents the conversion of proteins into fat.

Fats: Get rid of the misconception that you don't need fats in your diet.

Fats are essential in your diet, although they should be only the unsaturated fats and omega-3 and 6 fats. Below are some reasons why fat is so critical for us

- Fats provide energy
- They form cell membranes
- Some vitamins like vitamins A, E, D, and K need fat to absorb.

- They produce hormones.
- Fats form a layer beneath our skin, protecting muscles and, at the same time, providing warmth to our body.

Sources: Nuts and seeds. Replace your regular cooking oil with coconut oil, ground nut, or natural sesame seed oil.

- Vitamins And Minerals: These nutrients are essential for our body, although in smaller quantities than proteins and carbohydrates. Although in small amounts, they should be a part of our daily diet, and deficiency of any of them may lead to serious health problems.
- Fiber: Fibers are needed to normalize our bowel movements. They also help prevent chronic diseases like cardiovascular disease, cancer, and diabetes.
- Iron is an essential nutrient that helps maintain our hemoglobin level, develop brain cells, and increase concentration.
- Calcium: It develops teeth and bones and strengthens them, preventing fracture. Good calcium intake in our diet also prevents the chances of developing osteoporosis.

Many of us often eat high-calorie junk food after a busy schedule. But in the long run, this may negatively impact our overall health. However, there is always time to start the habit of healthy eating. Eating a well-balanced diet provides the required nutrients, improves the immune system, cuts down the risk of obesity, and ensures proper body functioning. A well-balanced diet includes balanced amounts of protein, carbohydrates, fats, vitamins, minerals, and fiber. Hence, try including foods rich in these nutrients to make your diet healthy and balanced.

An Essential element to lead energetic life

Want to feel better, have more energy, and even add years to your life? Just exercise. It boosts your energy, mood and stamina.

The health benefits of regular exercise and physical activity are hard to ignore. Everyone benefits from training, regardless of age, sex, or physical ability. Although exercise can lead to a happier and healthier life, there are different benefits of doing exercise.

Exercise controls weight:

Exercise can help prevent excess weight gain or help maintain weight loss. When you engage in physical activity, you burn calories. The more intense the training, the more calories you burn. Regular trips to the gym are great but don't worry if you can't find a large chunk of time to exercise every day. Any amount of activity is better than none at all. To reap the benefits of exercise, just get more active throughout your day — take the stairs instead of the elevator or rev up your household chores. Consistency is key.

Exercise combats health conditions and diseases

Worried about heart disease? Hoping to prevent high blood pressure? No matter your current weight, being active boosts high-density lipoprotein (HDL) cholesterol, the "good" cholesterol, and it decreases unhealthy triglycerides. This one-two punch keeps your blood flowing smoothly, reducing cardiovascular disease risk.

Regular exercise helps prevent or manage many health problems and concerns, including:

- Stroke
- Metabolic syndrome
- High blood pressure
- Type 2 diabetes
- Depression
- Anxiety
- Many types of cancer
- Arthritis
- Fall

It can also help improve cognitive function and helps lower the risk of death from all causes.

1. Exercise improves mood: Need an emotional lift? Or need to destress after a stressful day? A gym session or brisk walk can help. Physical activity stimulates various brain chemicals that may leave you feeling happier, more relaxed, and less anxious. You may also feel better about your appearance and yourself when you exercise regularly, which can boost your confidence and self-esteem.
2. Exercise boosts energy: Winded by grocery shopping or household chores? Regular physical activity can improve your muscle strength and increase your endurance. Training delivers oxygen and nutrients to your tissues and helps your cardiovascular system work more efficiently. And when your heart and lung health improve, you have more energy to tackle daily chores.
3. Exercise promotes better sleep: Struggling to snooze? Regular physical activity can help you fall asleep faster, get better, and deepen your sleep. Exercise only a little bit to bedtime or you may be too energized to sleep.
4. Exercise puts the spark back into your sex life: Do you feel too tired or too out of shape to enjoy physical intimacy? Regular physical activity can improve energy levels and increase your confidence in your physical appearance, which may boost your sex life. But there's even more to it than that. Regular physical activity may enhance arousal for women. And men who exercise regularly are less likely to have problems with erectile dysfunction than men who don't exercise.
5. Exercise can be fun and social: Exercise and physical activity can be enjoyable. It gives you a chance to unwind, enjoy the outdoors, or simply engage in activities that make you happy. Physical activity can also help you connect with family or friends in a fun social setting. So, take a dance class, hit the hiking trails, or join a soccer team. Find a physical activity you enjoy, and just do it. Try something new, or do something with friends or family. The bottom is Exercise and physical activity are great ways to feel better, boost your health, and have fun. For

most healthy adults, the U.S. Department of Health and Human Services recommends these exercise guidelines: **Aerobic activity.** Get at least 150 minutes of moderate aerobic activity or 75 minutes of vigorous aerobic activity a week, or a combination of moderate and vigorous activity. The guidelines suggest that you spread out this exercise over a week. To provide even more significant health benefits and to assist with weight loss or maintaining weight loss, at least 300 minutes a week is recommended. But even small amounts of physical activity are helpful. Being active for short periods throughout the day can provide health benefits. **Strength training.** Do strength training exercises for all major muscle groups at least two times a week. Aim to do a single set of each exercise using a heavy weight or resistance level to tire your muscles after about 12 to 15 repetitions.

Moderate aerobic exercise includes brisk walking, biking, swimming, and mowing the lawn. Vigorous aerobic exercise includes running, heavy yard work, and aerobic dancing. Strength training can consist of using weight machines, your own body weight, heavy bags, resistance tubing or resistance paddles in the water, or activities such as rock climbing. If you want to lose weight, meet specific fitness goals or get even more benefits, you should ramp up your moderate aerobic activity.

Remember to check with your doctor before starting a new exercise program, especially if you have any concerns about your fitness, haven't exercised for a long time, or have chronic health problems like heart disease, diabetes, or arthritis.

"We're all busy but it's not an excuse to sacrifice your health and fitness"

Call of Action: List down what are the areas you want to focus. For example: Losing weight, building muscle, Increasing Stamina, maintaining high energy levels, Medicine free life. It is important to keep a track on each radicle detail time to time by implementing and consuming these 5 elements. Work on root cause of any disease in natural way.

CHAPTER IX

Financial Management

"The number one problem in today's generation and economy is the lack of financial literacy"

By Alan Greenspan

We were taught to earn more money to lead a comfortable and happy life. However, we needed to be taught how to manage our Money or finances effectively. It is an important skill one must learn from schooling. It is equally important to learn tools and techniques to save or invest your hard-earned money in a productive way to successfully reach all your financial goals. Here I will not explain detailed financial planning or tools and techniques. Financial planning should be customized according to one's financial needs and goals. However, explain healthy financial habits in detail to help you.

Money is a necessary means to achieve many of your goals in life. Whether you want to go to college, buy a new car, or build a new home, having the proper finances will help you reach your objectives. Most of your financial needs are met by your Parents/guardians as students. As you graduate and come out of this comfort zone, the first obstacle you will face in the real world is managing your finances.

As you start your career, you start earning your own Money. Money that can buy your own clothes, food, bike/car, and whatnot? Money that helps establish your own name/identity; Money that can help you support your own family; Sounds nice. Isn't it? But what is Money?

MONEY Vs. FINANCE

What is Money?

Money is primarily a medium or means of exchange. It is a way for a person to trade what he has for what he wants. Ideal Money has three critical characteristics: it acts as a medium of exchange, an economic good, and a means of economic calculation.

"What is MONEY? A piece of PAPER, a chunk of METAL, or just some bits and bytes.

It's been called the ROOT OF ALL EVIL, but it can also help UPROOT ALL EVIL.

It can't buy you HAPPINESS or LOVE, but some fall in LOVE WITH IT anyway.

It can CHANGE who you are and help you find out WHO YOU really are.

It can ENSLAVE you and FREE you.

It can open DOORS, buy you DOORS, but it won't tell you what to do once you are INSIDE,

It can CONTROL you and give you CONTROL.

It can give you the power to say YES and the freedom to express NO.

It's EVERYTHING .... and NOTHING.

Because MONEY is just money."

What is Finance?

Many people often tend to believe that they control their Money. But many times, it is Money that actually holds people. It is a vicious trap! After all, people need to realize that Money is a RESOURCE. A resource that can help you fulfill your needs enables you to possess your wants, which can help you chase your dreams. A resource, if properly managed, can give you so much Joy and Happiness. When Money is viewed not as a medium of exchange but as a resource that can be managed, it is called FINANCE.

The Importance of Learning about Personal Finance

There are several reasons a person should learn about personal finance, but understandably, most people cannot see these reasons for themselves. Personal finance is a complex topic to learn about, so a person just naturally tends to shy away from it, making excuses to avoid knowing about it. Well, personal finance is significant, and here are some reasons why

Understand Money Flow

If you understand personal finance, you will realize your Money flow much better. Unfortunately, several people muddle through life in managing their expenses with their money and need help figuring out what to do with the surplus or deficit. These people have no idea how personal finance works, so even if they make the right decisions, they are doing it through luck.

Knowledge is power; if you know about your money flow, you arguably have the most essential individual ability today.

Remove Uncertainty and Fear

Human beings as a species have an irrational fear of uncertainty. In this respect, we are no different from any other mammalian species walking the planet because all of them have been conditioned through thousands of generations of being eaten and killed to be afraid of what they don't know. Therefore, uncertainty and fear go hand in hand. When they do this concerning something as crucial to your survival as Money, the paralyzing effect that fear can have on you is not even pleasant to think about.

Compare this situation to a situation where somebody knows how their money flow works and understands their entire personal finance situation. This person is not a person that is likely to be afraid since there is no uncertainty involved with their financial situation. It is a lot easier to be scared when you have no idea where your Money is coming from and where it is going.

Optimize Utilization:

If you genuinely understand personal finance, then another thing that you definitely should realize is Utilization. A person that does not understand or appreciate personal finance is a person that is unlikely to save a lot of money, instead spending whatever they happen to have left after monthly expenses on entertainment and impulse purchasing.

The Decision-Making Process:

To understand how our decision-making process affects our financial behavior, let us examine the following Case Study.

Case Study:

Your father gives you Rs.200 as pocket money. You are going out with your friends, and you come across your favorite fast-food joint. This is where you get your favorite food to eat; let us say your favorite Pizza costs Rs. 100.

The First question is: How many of you will order your favorite Pizza?

Let us assume that you and your friends order 1 Pizza each after paying Rs.100/-. Just when you are about to have your first bite, one of your friends hits you accidentally on your back, and you spill your Pizza on the floor.

The second question is: How many of you will order One More Pizza?

Now, if the same case study above is repeated with a slight twist, your father gave you Rs.200 pocket money in your Budget for 1 month.

The First question is: How many of you will order your favorite Pizza?

Now the second question is whether you will order One More Pizza after you lose your first Pizza?

If you are wondering why your decisions are different on the second instance, here is the explanation:

Imagine you have a pair of tiny twins living inside your head. Their names are Impulse and Logic. They do all of your thinking for you. All of your feeling, all your perceiving. They are in your mind, but there are two of them, and they couldn't be more different from each other.

Impulse and Logic

Impulse speaks no language, understands no words, and cannot reason. The girl has no sense of right or wrong. She wants gratification and avoids pain. She feels desire and fear. She is the ultimate pleasure seeker as well as the ultimate avoider of anything unpleasant. She is honest, straightforward, and lacks deception. She is pure passion, emotion, and impulse instinct. And she wants everything now!

Logic reads, writes, and does arithmetic. Logical and rational as the girl seeks facts, information, knowledge, and understanding. She makes unemotional judgments about good and evil, right and wrong, ethical and unethical, moral and immoral, and valuable and valueless. She thinks she reasons and judges but does not feel.

They are an interesting pair, these little twins. But the most exciting thing is that Impulse is the decision-maker of the two. Believe it or not, every decision you make is made by Impulse. That's right – the irrational one is making all of your choices. Unsettling, isn't it?

It's not that unsettling because Logic has a lot to say about it. The two of them work together productively. They both perceive through the senses; sight, sound, touch, smell, and taste. Logic takes whatever meaning is inherent in her perceptions and logically processes it. The result is passed along to Impulse, who interprets the results in terms of expected gratification or pain. And she reacts emotionally. Impulse provides the emotional response to Logic's rational conclusions and judgments. Meanwhile, Impulse also uses her sensory perceptions to make associations with past experiences, triggering decisions, while Impulse deals with associations and emotions.

The more information Logic can bring to judgments, the stronger her influence on the decisions. The key to healthy financial management is to provide more information and facts so that Logic can analyze and make the correct conclusion and judgment. This can be achieved by developing a systematic approach to making financial decisions.

1. Good Financial Habits to Develop:

a. Track your Spending

Keeping precise tabs on how much Money is coming in and going out of your checking account each month should be a top money priority. And we don't just mean estimating how much you "probably" spent on dinner or "about" how much you paid for your last vacation—we're talking exact numbers.

Bottom line: Knowing how much you've spent is necessary to know how much you have left toward critical financial goals, like building up your emergency fund and an excellent way to monitor your cash flow is to create a budget. Hence, at the start of each month, you know exactly how much money you have to allocate toward food, housing, student loans, lifestyle expenses, and future financial goals.

a. Live Below Your Means:

Put simply: Living below your means requires spending less money than you earn.

Easy enough, right?

In reality, many people understand the concept but need help with the execution. Once those regular expenses start catching up, it can be hard to keep your cash outflow less than your inflow.

Fortunately, a budget can do wonders for helping you live within your means. Once you have a solid framework for your monthly spending, it can be easier to see where you need to rein in any frivolous outflow.

c. Pay Yourself first:

Pay yourself first means Save First. People often commit the mistake of waiting for all expenses to get over so that they can save the remaining. But practically at the end of all costs, there is very little left for saving. So pay Yourself First. In the concept of Saving your amount at the beginning, say immediately after your inflow, so you can spend the remaining.

d. Save for the future:

Do you want to own a home one day? Have your own car? Travel to different countries? Start your own business? These goals can require serious cash—and now is the time to start getting it together.

Once you've identified your goals—and picked two or three to prioritize first—you can consider diverting Money into separate savings accounts. This not only helps you keep track of your savings progress, but it also helps curb any temptation to dip into one account to bolster another.

e. Distinguish Between Wants & Needs:

Needs: A need is something you have to have, something you can't do without.

Want - A want is something you would like to have. It is not absolutely necessary, but it would be a good thing to have.

On a global level, your basic needs are food, shelter, and transportation. But day to day, these will be different for everyone.

Case in point: A new pair of rain boots might be something you want if you already have a perfect pair at home, but it becomes necessary if your old pair has sprung a leak that soaks your socks on the walk to work

Clearly, a need takes priority over a want—so if you're looking to reduce your spending to put more money toward savings, your wants are the first place you should look to cut back. Of course, we're saying you can spend money on something other than your wants. But the sooner you can get in the habit of identifying which expenses are and aren't necessary, the easier it can be to modify your spending as you change your goals.

The 4-way Test:

The most common pitfall in personal finance is one's inability to contain the urge to spend. This is called Impulse Spending. Impulse Spending is nothing but a spur-of-the-moment, unplanned decision to buy, made just before a purchase.

Emotions and feelings play a decisive role in purchasing, triggered by seeing the product or upon exposure to a well-crafted promotional message. Such purchases range from small (chocolate, clothing, magazines) to substantially large (Jewelry, vehicle, work of art). Usually, they lead to problems such as financial difficulties, family disapproval, or feeling of guilt or disappointment.

As explained earlier, in our decision-making process, Logic brings rational conclusions and judgments. So, it is essential in any decision-making process to give ample opportunity for your Logic to process the situation and pass on the analysis to Impulse for a meaningful decision.

Here is a simple tool to put your Logic at work – The 4 ways Test. Before taking any major or minor financial decision, follow the four steps below. Then, ask yourself these questions to ensure that the conclusion you are going to make is logical and sensible.

Is that something you need/want?

Ensure that the thing that you are going to buy is something you need or want. If yes, move on to the next question. If no, then avoid your purchase and save it for the future.

Is it Important/Urgent?

Ensure whether the purchase is Important or Urgent. If yes, move on to the next question. If no, then avoid your purchase and postpone it for the future.

Does it add value to you?

Ensure whether the expense adds any value to you in terms of utility or otherwise. If yes, move on to the next question. If no, then avoid your purchase and save it for the future.

Does it fit in your Budget?

Ensure that the purchase is affordable to you and that it fits your pocket. If yes, move on and complete your purchase. If no, then avoid your purchase and save it for the future.

Eventually, building healthy financial habits will help you plan and lead your life more effectively. Be proactive and take charge of your financial destiny by building habits that could take you to greater peace and harmony in your life. Getting hold of these habits will help you in the future to achieve your goals and take care of yourself and your dear ones.

"Financial literacy not only involves the ability to count your money, it also tests your ability to evaluate the cost and benefit associated with each decision you make"

By Wayne Chirisa

Call of Action:Keep a separate budget book to track your finances. Allocate a specific percentage to every aspect, and check and recheck while you are tempting to spend. Whether budget permits or not.

CHAPTER X

Spirituality

"Spiritual development is not an accomplishment but a way of life. It is an orientation that brings its own rewards, and what is important is the direction of one's motives"

By David R. Hawkins

I started my spiritual journey at 33 and have observed many changes in my thoughts and happened to receive better clarity of what life is, and my responses to situations were changed. The outlook of my life has completely changed. Unfortunately, many of them have a misconception about spirituality. Although, as a part of my professional advancement, I have attended many pieces of training, I came to know all highly successful people in this world have a common trait: they are highly spiritual, and their works always serve humankind one way or another. Spirituality gives us clarity of our life purpose. Let me explain in detail. Spirituality is the broad concept of a belief in something beyond the self. It strives to answer questions about the meaning of life, how people are connected to each other, truths about the universe, and other mysteries of human existence.

Spirituality offers a worldview that suggests there is more to life than just what people experience on a sensory and physical level. Instead, it indicates that something greater connects all beings to each other and to the universe itself.

It may involve religious traditions centering on the belief in a higher power. However, it can also apply a holistic view of an individual connecting to others and the world.

Spirituality has been a source of comfort and relief from stress for multitudes of people. While people use many different paths to find God or a higher power, research has shown that those who are more religious or spiritual and use their spirituality to cope with challenges in life experience many benefits in their health and well-being.

Signs of Spirituality

Spirituality is not a single path or belief system. There are many ways to experience spirituality and the benefits of a spiritual experience. How you define spirituality will vary. For some people, it's the belief in a higher power or a specific religious practice.

For others, it may involve experiencing a connection to a higher state or inter-connectedness with the rest of humanity and nature.

Some signs of spirituality can include:

- Asking profound questions about topics such as suffering or what happens after death
- Deepening connections with other people
- Experiencing compassion and empathy for others
- Experiencing feelings of interconnectedness
- Feelings of awe and wonder
- Seeking happiness beyond material possessions or other external rewards
- Seeking meaning and purpose
- Wanting to make the world a better place

Not everyone experiences or expresses spirituality in the same way. Some people may seek spiritual experiences in every aspect of their lives, while others may be more likely to have these feelings under specific conditions or in certain locations only. For example, some people may be more likely to have spiritual experiences in churches or other religious temples, while others might have these feelings when they're out enjoying nature.

Types of Spirituality

There are many different types of spirituality. Some examples of how people get in touch with their own spirituality include:

- Breathwork
- Meditation or quiet time
- New age spirituality
- Prayer
- Service to their community
- Spending time in nature
- Spiritual retreats
- Yoga

Other people express their spirituality through religious traditions such as:

- Buddhism
- Christianity
- Hinduism
- Humanism
- Islam
- Judaism
- Sikhism

It is important to remember that many other spiritual traditions exist worldwide, including traditional African, Asian, American and Indigenous spiritual practices. Such spiritual practices can be essential to groups of people subjected to colonialism's effects.

Difference Between Spirituality and Religion

Though there can be a lot of overlap between spiritual people and religious people, below are some key points to help differentiate spirituality from religion.

Spirituality

- Can be practiced individually
- Doesn't have to adhere to a specific set of rules
- Often focuses on a personal journey of discovering what is meaningful in life

Religion

- Often practiced in a community
- Usually based on a specific set of rules and customs
- Often focuses on the belief in deities or gods, religious texts, and traditions

Uses of Spirituality

There are many different reasons why people may turn to spirituality, including but not limited to the following:

- **To find purpose and meaning**: Exploring spirituality can help people answer their philosophical questions, such as "What is the meaning of life?" and "What purpose does my life serve?"
- **To cope with feelings of stress, depression, and anxiety**: Spiritual experiences can be helpful when dealing with the stresses of life.
- **To restore hope and optimism**: Spirituality can help people develop a more hopeful outlook on life.
- **To find a sense of community and support**: Because spiritual traditions often involve organized religions or groups, becoming a part of such a group can serve as an essential source of social support.

Impact of Spirituality

While specific spiritual views are a matter of faith, research has demonstrated some benefits of spirituality and spiritual activity. The results may surprise no one who has found comfort in their religious or spiritual views. Still, they are definitely noteworthy in that they demonstrate in a scientific way that these activities do have benefits for many people.

The following are a few more of the many positive findings related to spirituality and health:

- Research has shown that religion and spirituality can help people cope with the effects of everyday stress. One study found that everyday spiritual experiences helped older adults cope with negative and enhanced positive feelings.
- Research shows that older women are more grateful to God than older men and receive greater stress-buffering health effects due to this gratitude.
- According to research, those with an intrinsic religious orientation, regardless of gender, exhibited less physiological reactivity toward stress than those with an extrinsic religious orientation. Those who were intrinsically oriented dedicated their lives to God or a "higher power," while the extrinsically oriented ones used religion for external ends like making friends or increasing community social standing.

This, along with other research, demonstrates that there may be tangible and lasting benefits to maintaining involvement with a spiritual community. This involvement, along with the gratitude that can accompany spirituality, can be a buffer against stress and is linked to greater levels of physical health.

Dedication to God or a higher power translated into less stress reactivity, greater feelings of well-being, and ultimately even a decreased fear of death.

People who feel comfortable and comforted using spirituality as a coping mechanism for stress can rest assured that there's even more evidence that this is a good idea for them. Prayer works for young and old alike. Prayer and spirituality have been linked to:

- Better Health
- Greater psychological well-being
- Less depression
- Less hypertension
- Less stress, even during difficult times
- More positive feelings
- Superior ability to handle stress

How to Become More Mindful in Your Everyday Life:

Practice Spirituality: Whether you are rediscovering a forgotten spiritual path, reinforcing your commitment to an already well-established one, or learning more about spirituality for beginners, there are countless ways to start exploring your spiritual side and help improve your well-being.

Spirituality is a personal experience, and everyone's spiritual path may be unique. Research shows, however, that some spiritual stress relief strategies have been helpful to many, regardless of faith. Some things you can do to start exploring spirituality include:

- Pay attention to how you feel: Part of embracing spirituality is embracing what it means to be human, both the good and the bad.
- Focus on others: Opening your heart, feeling empathy, and helping others are important aspects of spirituality.
- Meditate: Try spending 10 to 15 minutes each morning engaged in meditation.
- Practice gratitude: Start a gratitude journal and record what you are grateful for daily. This can be a great reminder of what is most important to you and what brings you the greatest happiness.

- Try mindfulness: By becoming more mindful, you can become more aware and appreciative of the present. Mindfulness encourages you to be less judgmental (both of yourself and others) and focus more on the present moment rather than dwelling on the past or future.

Be Cautious about spiritual bypassing:

One potential pitfall of spirituality is a phenomenon known as spiritual bypassing. This involves a tendency to use spirituality to avoid or sidestep problems, emotions, or conflicts.

For example, rather than apologizing for some emotional wound you have caused someone else, you might bypass the problem by simply excusing it and saying that "everything happens for a reason" or suggesting that the other person just needs to "focus on the positive."

Spirituality can enrich your life and lead to several benefits. Still, it is essential to be cautious to not let spiritual ideals lead to pitfalls such as dogmatism or a reason to ignore the needs of others.

"Spiritual life does not remove us from the world but leads us deeper into it"

***By Henri* J.M. Nouwen**

Call of Action: Be silent for some time connecting to your own self, once in a while. Listen to spiritual speeches every now and then.

CHAPTER XI

Visualization

"When you visualize, then you materialize"

Let's talk about the scientific power of thought, some scientists experimented on the strength of imagination with two groups of people. One group did muscle-building exercises for 4 weeks, while the others just imagined doing it. Astonishingly, this last group still managed to increase their muscle strength by a whopping 22%.

According to the scientists involved, this is due to the neurons deep within the human brain still being used and strengthened for muscle-building instructions. Neurons are nerve cells that transmit and process information in the brain. They are highly excitable, sending out electrical and chemical signals to other cells in your body – like the cells in the muscles - at lightning speeds. Amazingly, the brain has around 100 billion neurons, averaging about 5,000 connections each, similar to having 500 trillion microprocessors wired together in a single network. Our brain is truly an excellent machine, no doubt – a natural resource inside your skull right now.

In another study, similar test results were found with pianists. A group imagining their piano practice for two hours a day still achieved positive results in their playing abilities. The same physical changes in the brain still occurred, specifically in the motor cortex region. However, I emphasize that the participants involved were all competent pianists in the first place.

On a serious note, just think of all the things you can achieve with willpower? Your imaginative mind can harness the power of your natural gifts: your skills, talents, and unique brain. Additionally, it can do this even under the most difficult of circumstances.

Why not use your imagination to make your dreams come true.

The tool is called visualization. If we keep practicing and visualize/imagining what we want in our life to be achieved, it will come one day as reality. They are many proven stories available on google.

Anything in this universe is made twice, "once in the human mind and once in reality." We use things like bulbs, telephones, computers, mixers, grinders, fans, AC, cars, bikes.... etc. What not, once it was not existing. Everything is created by man's mind.

Hence, start visualizing twice a day as soon you wake up and before going to bed about your dreams/ goals in relationships, career, health, money, travel, achievements, success, spirituality, and anything you want to achieve.

"Dare to visualize a world in which your most treasured dreams have become true"

By Ralph Marsto

Call of Action: Write down all your Goals/ Dreams to achieve in your life create a pictorial presentation. Look at it whenever is possible repeatedly.

My life Journey

"All the qualities and character traits a person persist are the seeds sown in childhood"

My first nerve wrecking experience in life is at the age of 3 and I have only heard stories about it. I was diagnosed with an unknown disease, while was deadly and even a saline needle cannot be inserted. At the very same time a doctor who was considered a psych saved me by injecting a medicine into the last nerve in a body i.e., at feet and only then I recovered and got saved.

At the age of 7 my grandmother shown me the way to devotion and the idea of GOD and with that I was completely submerged into it by chanting and praying. Group of sadhus watching me wanted me to join them and become a servant to GOD. But my parents could not give me up. This sown the seed of spirituality in me.

I was a very shy girl to begin with. In my entire schooling and college, I did not have many friends and cared only about my grades. In summer I used to learn a new skill like learning Hindi, sewing and stitching, Type writing, Bhagwat Gita, Singing classes, Shloka classes etc. Even though these were the classes my mother joined me in, later on "The seed of learning was sown"

At the age of 18, I was married to my Husband Ramesh. Few first years of married life were full of roses but later on I had to walk on the thorns. Few months after giving birth to my first born, my husband had to separate from the family business due to financial issues between my husband and my father-in-law. That was when my husband has started his own business with the Gold that was given to me by my parents for marriage and that was not the end. I wanted to complete my degree as my marriage was done in between, I have not received any help from my husband or In-laws. At that moment my parents stepped in and taken care of the fees and also my child. Later on my hard work paid as I passed the exams in first class. During my second pregnancy my In-laws would not even give me food as I was not doing any work in the house and that lead to a near abortion. I then left my In-laws house and went back to my parents' house and with god's grace I have given birth to a healthy baby. Later on, issues have continued at my In-laws and had to leave the house with only the clothes we wore.

After separation we have struggled to streamline my husband's business. Me and my husband had many sleepless nights and were working day by day to steady the business and make it stand on its own and this took us five years. Later on, after our business was stabilized, I joined corporate as a financial advisor. After one year I was promoted to financial trainer in the same organization. Later on, after few years I was completely torn apart because of family challenges and left my career. We were facing a lot of legal issues due to my father-in-law. We did not have enough money to afford a lawyer and other legal costs. All these made me turn supreme power again and from then on driven spiritually. After starting spiritual journey, I found peace internally. It has given me strength to start my career in finance field again. I understood that my knowledge should be expanded for flourishing in the industry and acquired many certifications from reputed organizations in financial markets. I started freelancing while pursuing my MBA completely funded by myself. I was climbing up in my carrier managing and juggling between different roles.

Year 2012, I have quit my job to support my children in their education. I was handling my kids alongside started my own business. After 3 years of successfully running it, I did not find happiness in it and quit the business by handing it over to my friend. This time I have started my training journey as a soft skills trainer rather than financial trainer and this profile shift took me a year and I've never looked back.

Year 2020 pandemic hit and I discovered Law of attraction and that is when I realized the practices done by me in spiritual life were proven scientifically. All the aspects I learned in spiritual life were making sense to me more than ever. I have mixed my core strength and spiritual strength backed up with Law of attraction and started my venture called “Redesign your Life”.

Year 2022 I have lost both my parents. The trauma of losing both of them in six months gap made me write this book and honor it in their name. All the financial certification done in my career made me win national ward in PERSONAL FINANCIAL PLANNING which increased my responsibility and I intend to continue serving women by educating them financially and spiritually.

Dear Reader,

I have tried to keep this book error free. But if errors have crept in, do let me know. The images used in this book are sourced from Google.

Thank you for buying this book

9 798888 695135

Printed by Libri Plureos GmbH in Hamburg,
Germany